Texas Joins the United States

Christy Steele

WORLD ALMANAC® LIBRARY

Please visit our web site at: www.worldalmanaclibrary.com
For a free color catalog describing World Almanac® Library's list of high-quality books and multimedia programs, call 1-800-848-2928 (USA) or 1-800-387-3178 (Canada). World Almanac® Library's fax: (414) 332-3567.

Library of Congress Cataloging-in-Publication Data

Steele, Christy, 1970-
Texas joins the United States / by Christy Steele.
p. cm. — (America's westward expansion)
Includes bibliographical references and index.
ISBN 0-8368-5791-7 (lib. bdg.)
ISBN 0-8368-5798-4 (softcover)
1. Texas—History—To 1846—Juvenile literature. 2. Texas—History—Revolution, 1835-1836—Juvenile literature. 3. Texas—History—Republic, 1836-1846—Juvenile literature. 4. United States—Territorial expansion—Juvenile literature. I. Title.
F386.3.S725 2005
976.4'01—dc22 2004056771

First published in 2005 by
World Almanac® Library
330 West Olive Street, Suite 100
Milwaukee, WI 53212 USA

Produced by: EMC—The Education Matters Company
Editors: Christy Steele, Rachael Taaffe
Designer and page production: Jennifer Pfeiffer
Maps and diagrams: Jennifer Pfèiffer
World Almanac® Library editorial direction: Mark J. Sachner
World Almanac® Library art direction: Tammy West
World Almanac® Library production: Jessica Morris
World Almanac® Library editors: Monica Rausch, Carol Ryback

Photo credits: Corbis, 10, 24; East Texas Research Center at Stephen F. Austin State University, 16; Library of Congress: cover, 4, 5, 6, 9, 22, 28, 30, 32, 33, 34, 36, 39, 40, 41; National Archives: 11, 13, 23, 35, 43; North Wind Picture Archives, 17, 19; Texas State Library & Archives: 18, 29; Texas State Preservation Board: 14, 21, 27.

Printed in Canada

1 2 3 4 5 6 7 8 9 09 08 07 06 05

Contents

Texas—from New Spain to Mexico

The era of U.S. westward expansion is generally described as having lasted from 1803, when the United States acquired a huge amount of land from France in the Louisiana Purchase, until about 1912. During this era, U.S. land policy was shaped by the belief in "Manifest Destiny." Writer John O'Sullivan first used this term in 1845 to explain the idea that God had given Americans the right to take over the continent and spread U.S. ideas and government to new peoples and territories. The United States completed its Manifest Destiny by purchasing or conquering territory and taking land from Native peoples until its borders stretched from coast to coast.

◀ John Gast's 1872 painting, *American Progress,* represented the American ideal of Manifest Destiny. It shows an angel named Liberty traveling west with American settlers, stringing a telegraph wire behind them.

Hoping for riches, land, or adventure, thousands of Americans listened to an 1851 quote of John Soule's, which was popularized by famous newspaper owner Horace Greeley: "Go West, young man, and grow up with the country." By 1850, an estimated 4 million pioneers had left established states along the East Coast to settle new U.S. territory in the West. Immigrants in search of land or gold poured into the United States from around the world. From 1812 to 1850, the U.S. population increased from about 7.25 million to 23 million.

Texas was an important part of U.S. westward expansion. When it became a state, Texas added valuable resources, a large amount of territory, and a diverse mix of people with a rich cultural heritage to the United States.

Texas and New Spain

For thousands of years, Native American groups, such as the Comanche and Apache, lived in the area now known as Texas. Most American Indians lived in small family groups that moved with the seasons to hunt, fish, trade, and farm.

Beginning in 1519, Texas was part of "New Spain," the Spanish-owned area of the Americas that also included present-day Florida, Mexico, New Mexico, Arizona, and California. People called the central portion of New Spain "Mexico" and referred to the northern frontier area of Mexico as Texas.

From 1682 to 1793, Spain cemented its hold on Texas by building about

▼ Ruins of the Mission San Jose y San Miguel de Aguayo pictured in 1933 in San Antonio, Texas. Mission Indians had to leave their traditional homes and live in these small apartments.

▲ Hacienda Cardenas headquarters in Mexico in 1880s. Large haciendas like this were used for ranching, farming, mining, or lumber. They could be like small towns with shops, living quarters, and even a church.

twenty-six missions there. Priests in these large church complexes forced Native Americans to convert to Catholicism and used the converts as slave labor on mission ranches and farms.

The Spanish also granted large tracts of land to a few wealthy, upper-class Spaniards, known as *patróns*, for creating huge business estates called *haciendas*. Patróns used African slaves or hired cowhands to mine or to raise cattle, horses, and goats. Spaniards who were not as wealthy received smaller land grants to form smaller ranches called *ranchos*. Ranchos were worked mainly by the ranchero and his family.

Some Native American groups in Texas resisted Spanish rule and raided missions, haciendas, and rancheros. To protect its frontier, Spain built several presidios, which were military forts staffed with soldiers.

A diverse mix of people lived in Texas, including Spaniards, Native Americans, colonists from the Canary Islands, and mestizos—people of both Native American and Spanish descent. Texans who had descended from Indian groups native to northern Mexico called themselves Tejanos.

Mexican War of Independence

In 1810, colonists in the North American portions of New Spain, in present-day Mexico and the U.S. Southwest, wanted freedom from Spain and rebelled. Several important battles of this Mexican War of Independence (1810–1821) took place in Texas.

In January 1811, Manuel Salcedo, the Spanish-appointed governor of Texas, discovered that Mexican revolutionaries near the Rio Grande River were trying to escape into the United States. The governor ordered his men to stop the revolutionaries. Instead, military leader Juan Bautista de las Casas led his soldiers in a revolt. They imprisoned Governor Salcedo and declared themselves part of the Mexican War of Independence.

Some of Casas's soldiers, however, were unhappy with his leadership and started a rumor that he worked for France. San Antonio residents switched their loyalty back to Spain and ousted the revolutionaries in March 1811. Casas was beheaded by Spanish troops, and Texas was once again under Spanish rule.

In 1812, Americans who supported the revolutionary

Spanish Influences on Texas

When Texas was Spanish property (1519–1821), it linked Spain's Southwest, Mexico, and Florida territories. When French explorers began descending from French-owned Canada down the Mississippi River to the Gulf of Mexico in the 1700s, Spanish officials worried that France would try to claim the Texas area, thus separating Florida from the rest of New Spain and gaining access to the riches of Spain's nearby New Mexico silver mines. Spanish officials tried to keep the French away from their territory by colonizing Texas with loyal Spanish citizens.

The Spanish settlers in Texas created a powerful Hispanic cultural legacy that still exists today. The Spanish language is widely spoken in Texas, with hundreds of cities, landmarks, and geographical features bearing Spanish names. Spanish art, mission architecture, and food are common in the area. The Spanish introduced horses, goats, and sugarcane to Texas. Property rights and water law were influenced by the Spanish legal system, and the mission system affected the development of farming and ranching techniques.

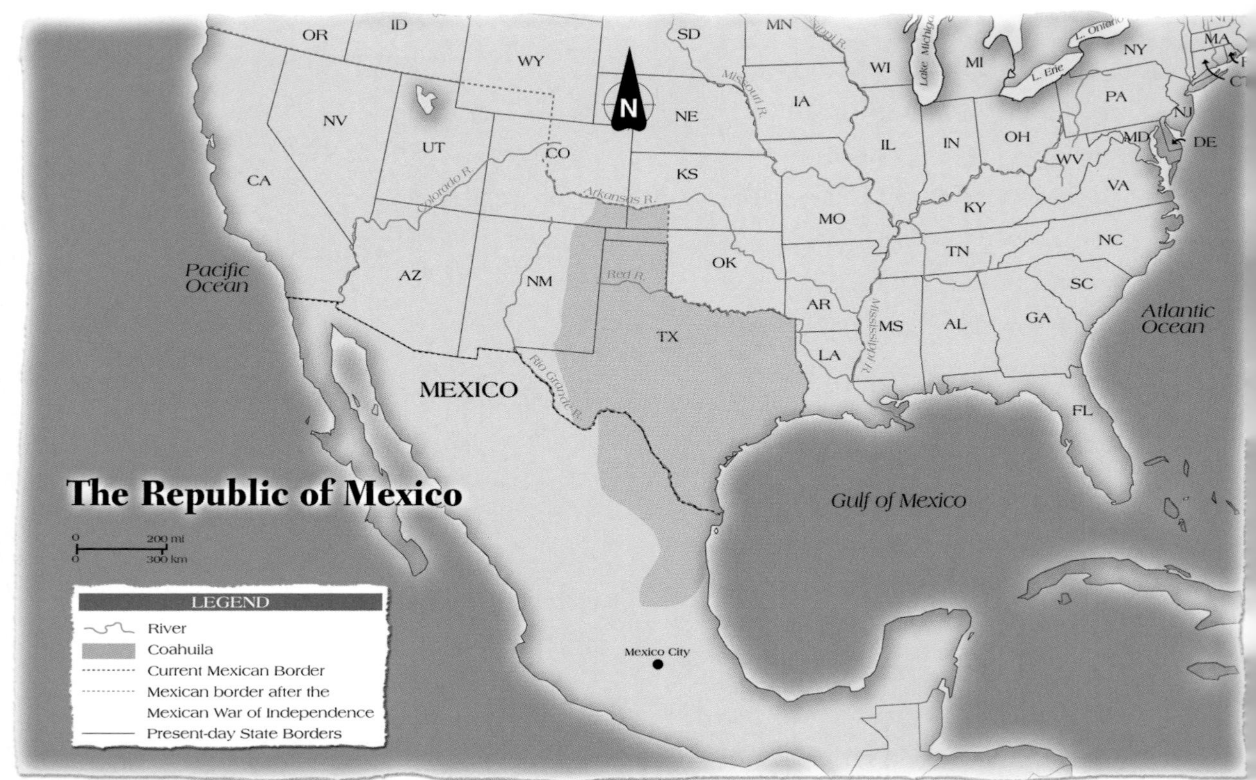

▲ This map shows the boundaries of the Republic of Mexico after the Mexican War of Independence. Texas was a northern frontier province of Mexico and was part of the state of Coahuila.

cause funded the Gutiérrez-Magee Expedition. With money from U.S. backers, an army led by José Bernardo Gutiérrez de Lara and Augustus William Magee marched from Louisiana to Texas on August 7, 1812. The expedition's soldiers quickly conquered several towns and executed Spanish leaders, including Governor Salcedo. On April 6, 1813, Gutiérrez declared that Texas was a free republic. Spain disagreed and assembled an army of about 1,830 soldiers. On August 18, 1813, the two armies fought the Battle of Medina near San Antonio. During the bloodiest battle on Texas soil, more than 1,000 members of the Gutiérrez-Magee Expedition were killed, and Spain assumed control of Texas again.

From 1815 to 1820, only a few small bands of rebels continued the fight for independence. In 1821, the Spanish sent

Agustín de Iturbide to fight one of these rebel groups, but news of a revolt back in Spain made Iturbide and his army change sides. He convinced rebel bands to unite under his leadership. This huge army soon outnumbered Spanish forces, and the Spanish viceroy resigned without fighting. Finally, on August 24, 1821, Spain granted Mexico independence.

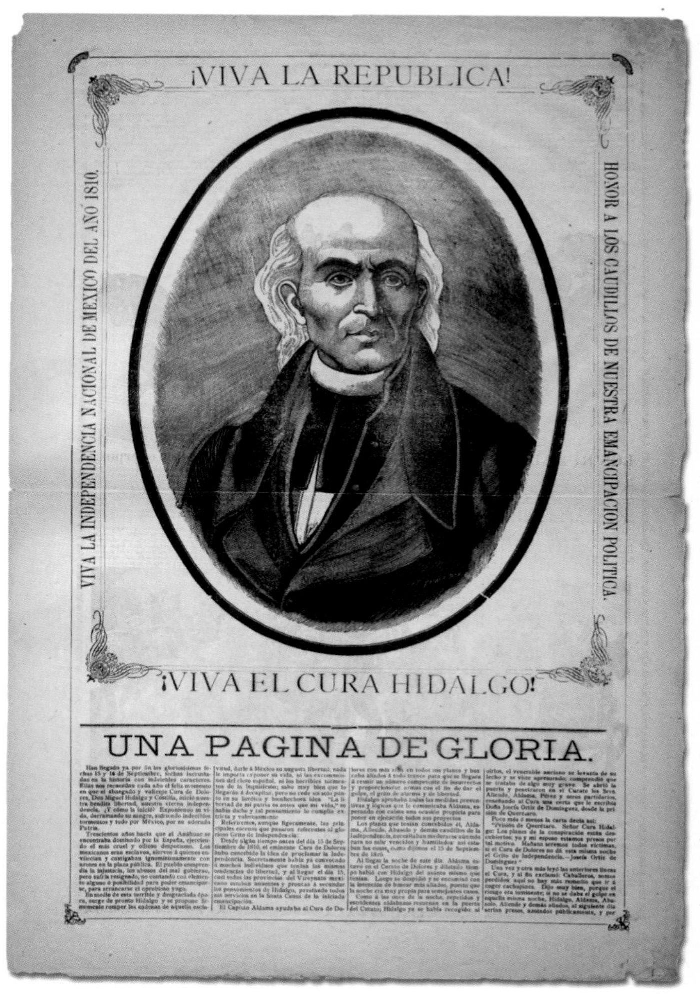

▲ Father Miguel Hidalgo y Costilla. In his famous Grito de Dolores speech, he called for Mexico's freedom from Spain. Hidalgo then organized the first Mexican army and led it in fights against the Spanish. Hidalgo was killed by Spanish troops.

Mexican Texas

Tejanos swore allegiance to the new nation of Mexico, but politics in Mexico's early years were highly changeable and violent. Two main groups, Federalists and Centralists, fought each other during several civil wars. Federalists wanted a government of self-governing states loosely controlled by a federal government. Centralists wanted weak states ruled by a strong central authority.

At first, Centralists controlled the country, but in 1824, Federalists assumed power and wrote a constitution that granted more power to individual Mexican states. Texas was made part of the state of Coahuila.

Settlement in Mexican Texas

Before the Mexican War of Independence, Texas was a slowly growing frontier province. By 1821, the population had declined to about 2,500 because many Texans were killed during the war. Mexico did not have enough population to settle the area, so it tried to attract foreign settlers with an appealing colonization policy.

Colonization in Mexican Texas

Leaders of the Mexican state of Coahuila, which controlled settlement in Texas, passed the State Colonization Law on March 25, 1825. In the law, Coahuila leaders declared that U.S. citizens were welcome to settle in the state, but Mexicans would receive first

◀ Illustration of Stephen Austin (right) and a Mexican land official (seated) officially assigning land to colonists at a gathering by the Colorado River in Texas in 1823.

choice of land. To attract newcomers, settlers were excused from paying taxes for ten years. The heads of households—male or female—could cheaply purchase a land grant consisting of one *sitio* (4,428 acres or 1,792 hectares) of land to graze livestock and a *labor* (177 acres or 72 ha) of land for farming. In exchange, settlers had to promise to practice the Christian religion, exhibit good conduct, and obey the laws of Mexico. Mexico also secularized Spanish missions; it took control from the church and granted or sold mission land to individuals.

▲ The Shoshone at Fort Washakie Indian reservation in Wyoming in 1892. Many Native Americans from the East who did not move to Texas to escape the U.S. government's relocation policy ended up on reservations.

Some of the first emigrants to Texas were Native American groups from the eastern United States. After the Louisiana Purchase in 1803, the U.S. government began forcibly removing Native American groups from their traditional homelands and resettling them in the newly purchased territory. To escape the U.S. government, some American Indian groups, such as the Cherokee (Keetoowha), Chickasaw, and Chocktaw, moved to Mexican Texas.

Anglo Americans, or Americans of non-Hispanic European descent, seeking bargain land moved to Mexico by the thousands. U.S. land cost about $1.25 per acre (.4 ha), while land in Mexican Texas cost about 4 cents per acre (.4 ha).

Slavery in Mexican Texas

Mexico's constitution outlawed slavery. Stephen Austin, the founder of Texas's first major Anglo colony, however, argued that Southern settlers would not come to Texas unless they could bring their slaves to work the rich land, so the Mexican government granted permission for slavery in the Texas territory. Even so, the Mexican government did not allow the buying or selling of slaves in Mexico. Mexican officials also periodically implied that they might reverse their exception of allowing slavery in Texas and outlaw slavery there, too. Even the suggestion that slavery might be outlawed caused conflict with the Anglo settlers who wanted to keep slaves.

Slavery slowly spread throughout the eastern two-thirds of Texas, especially near rivers where cotton and sugarcane grew easily in the rich soil.

In 1836, there were about 5,000 African American slaves in Texas. With the expansion of large Anglo cotton plantations, census records show that the number of slaves increased to about 58,100 by 1850 and to about 182,500 by 1860.

Texas Economy

Although trappers roamed the Texas area to hunt otters, beavers, deer, and bears, ranching and farming were the most popular methods of earning a living on the Texas frontier. Ranch owners raised cattle, swine, horses, and sheep, and farms growing cotton, corn, wheat, sugarcane, and tobacco dotted the landscape. To feed their families, settlers irrigated small fields and grew vegetable and fruit gardens. Cotton was the main export crop, and an 1834 report estimated that seven thousand bales of Texas cotton worth about $315,000 sold in New Orleans.

When they needed supplies, settlers traveled from their farms to towns or trading posts, a distance of hundreds of miles in some cases. Currency was scarce in Texas, and much of it was counterfeit, so most business was conducted by bartering—trading one item for another—such as pigs for medical care or corn for clothing.

Empresario System

Most settlers negotiated land deals through immigration agents called *empresarios*. Empresarios bought large land contracts from the Mexican government for select places. Their contract required them to settle a certain number of qualified families and make sure their settlers obeyed the laws of Mexico. Between 1821 and 1835, Mexican officials awarded forty-one empresario grants.

Empresarios advertised in the United States or abroad for families to populate their settlements. For each one hundred families settled, empresarios received a bonus of 23,000 acres (9,308 ha). Mexico then sent a land commissioner to issue deeds to the settlers. Settlers had to pay additional deed-processing fees to the Mexican government as well as to the land commissioner, the surveyor, and the clerk. Some settlers were never able to afford the formal deed to their land.

▲ Empresarios wanted to begin their colonies on the best possible land, in order to attract more settlers. Many chose land near the Rio Grande, shown here in 1890. Steamboats carried goods from the colonies down the river to markets.

Sometimes the government sold the same land to two empresarios, which caused lengthy legal conflicts. Some empresarios illegally sold land grants they did not own to land companies, and the land companies then sold property from these fraudulent grants to pioneers, leaving no land for the pioneers to legally settle on when they arrived in Texas.

▼ Stephen Austin, known as the "Father of Texas" because of his colonization efforts and role in the Texas Revolution, devoted his life to Texas. In a letter written just before his death, he noted that "The prosperity of Texas has been the object of my labors, the idol of my existence."

Stephen Austin

Stephen Austin was the most successful empresario, even though colonizing Texas was his father's idea. In 1820, Moses Austin received a colonization contract to settle three hundred Catholic families to farm sugarcane and cotton. He settled several families in Mexico, but died in 1821 without completing his contract.

In 1822, Stephen Austin visited Mexico City, Mexico's capital, to ask permission to continue his father's colonization contract. In 1823, officials gave Austin permission to continue settling his father's colony.

As an empresario, Austin was in charge of law and order in his colony. Settlers elected local justices of the peace, and Austin served as the superior judge and head of the militia. He also negotiated trade agreements and treaties with local Native American groups.

By 1828, the population in San Felipe, the capital of Austin's

Unsurpassed Soil and Immigrant Bounties in Texas

—Address given by Stephen Austin in Kentucky on March 7, 1836.

"We have one of the finest countries in the world, a soil surpassed by none for agriculture and pasturage, not even by the fairest portions of Kentucky—a climate that may be compared to Italy; within the cotton or sugar region, intersected by navigable rivers, and bounded by the Gulf of Mexico, on which there are several fine bays and harbors suitable for all the purposes of commerce—a population of about seventy thousand, which is rapidly increasing, and is composed of men of very reputable education and property, enterprising, bold and energetic, devotedly attached to liberty and their country, inured to the exercise of arms, and at all times ready to use them, and defend their homes inch by inch if necessary. The exportations of cotton are large. Cattle, sheep and hogs are very abundant and cheap. The revenue from importations and direct taxes will be considerable, and rapidly increasing; the vacant lands are very extensive and valuable, and may be safely relied upon as a great source of revenue and as bounties to emigrants."

colony, was large enough for Mexico to organize an official *ayuntamiento.* The ayuntamiento was like a town council, and its elected members settled lawsuits and controlled colony business, such as fixing roads, establishing schools, and regulating the welfare of its residents by supervising doctors and lawyers.

Austin's colony started the first newspaper in Texas, the *Texas Gazette.* Besides reporting news, the newspaper explained Mexican laws and the policies of Austin's colony to the settlers.

By 1834, Austin had settled nine hundred sixty-six families and formed seven of the largest Anglo communities in Texas. By 1835, there were about twenty thousand Anglo colonists in Texas and only about five thousand Mexicans. The number of settlements had grown from three, when Mexico first gained independence, to twenty-one—most founded by Anglos. The Anglos wanted more influence and wanted to participate in shaping the decisions of their government, which began causing conflicts with Mexican officials who did not want to share power.

Texas Revolution

Conflicts between Mexico and Anglo settlers intensified in 1826. That year, Mexico canceled an empresario contract with Haden Edwards. Edwards did not want to lose the $50,000 he already had invested in the colony, so he separated from Mexico with his colonists. He signed a Declaration of Independence and formed the Republic of Fredonia on December 21, 1826. On January 31, 1827, Austin's colony militia and Mexican troops ended the short-lived Republic of Fredonia.

Mexican officials—worried that other Anglo Texans would be inspired to separate from Mexico—passed a law in 1830 prohibiting further Anglo American settlement. The government also decided to add bases and send more

◀ Haden Edwards made an alliance with Cherokee Indians to support the Fredonian Rebellion, but fled to Louisiana at the first sign of an armed conflict with Mexico. He eventually returned to Texas and lived there for the rest of his life.

troops to guard the area. The free tariff period had also expired for settlers, and the government wanted the soldiers to collect taxes.

Turtle Bayou Resolution

In 1832, the first large battle between Anglo Texans and Mexican troops broke out in Velasco. The conflict began when Mexican commander John Bradburn arrested two Anglo Texans whom he accused of starting a riot. He held the settlers in prison without regard to the rule of Mexican law. The Battle of Velasco broke out when about one hundred fifty men sailed into the Gulf of Mexico to free the two imprisoned settlers. Mexican troops tried to stop the Texas rescue force, and the Texans attacked the fort. The commander of Fort Velasco surrendered and Bradburn was removed from command. Other Texas settlements also acted to remove Mexican troops from local forts.

▲ Antonio López de Santa Anna, shown here in an artist's sketch, started his political career as a Federalist. He later became a Centralist and ruled Mexico as a dictator.

Meanwhile, Centralists and Federalists in Mexico were fighting a civil war. Texans wrote the Turtle Bayou Resolutions to explain that they had only acted to remove the forces of President Bustamante, a Centralist, from Texas, so that Antonio López de Santa Anna, a Federalist at the time, could take control of the country's government. Santa Anna won the civil war, and Texans were not punished for their actions.

In 1832 and 1833, Texas leaders held conventions. At these meetings, they wrote a state constitution and a list of requests for the Mexican government, which included granting Texas Mexican statehood, reestablishing freedom from tariffs, and allowing

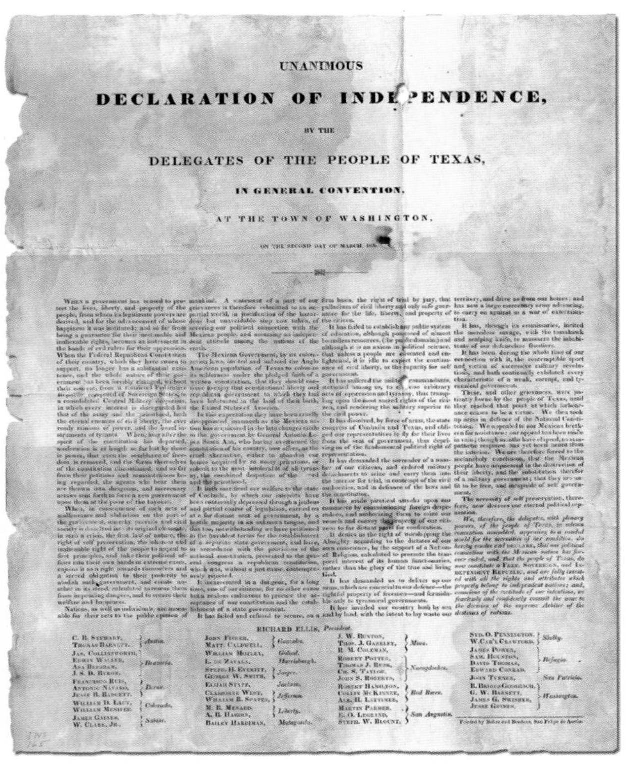
UNANIMOUS

DECLARATION OF INDEPENDENCE,

BY THE

DELEGATES OF THE PEOPLE OF TEXAS,

IN GENERAL CONVENTION,

AT THE TOWN OF WASHINGTON,

ON THE SECOND DAY OF MARCH, 1836.

RICHARD ELLIS, President.

▲ The Consultation passed a Declaration of Independence on November 7, 1835. Printed copies, such as this one, were posted throughout the region. The declaration stated that Texas was fighting the war in order to restore the Mexican Constitution of 1824 and achieve separate Mexican statehood for Texas.

more Anglo settlement. In 1833, the Mexican government granted the tariff request and overturned the 1830 law prohibiting Anglo settlement, but it did not grant separate statehood for Texas.

Texas Revolution

By 1835, Santa Anna had thrown out the 1824 Mexican constitution. He planned to show his authority by sending troops to the Texas forts that the Mexican army was forced to evacuate in 1832. In September, Santa Anna sent Mexican general Martín de Cos to Texas with five hundred troops.

Most Anglo Texans disapproved of Mexican laws. They did not support Santa Anna's changes to Mexico's government and did not want his Mexican troops in Texas. They were worried that he would use his troops to rule them like a tyrant. Anglo colonists formed the Consultation of 1835, a committee Texans organized to make Texas a separate state of Mexico, and made Stephen Austin its chairman. Texans felt they would have more control if Texas was its own state.

Tensions continued to rise between the Anglos and Santa Anna, however, and the first battle of the Texas Revolution (1835–1836) happened on October 2, 1835. Mexican troops from Béxar marched to Gonzales to reclaim a cannon lent to the colonists. Instead of surrendering the weapon, the Texans pointed to the cannon's location behind them and told the Mexican soldiers, "There it is—come and take it." When Mexican troops advanced toward the cannon, the Anglos fired it at them. The Mexican commander retreated.

On October 10, Stephen Austin assembled his colony's militia and marched with other volunteers—known as the Texas Army—to battle Cos's forces. In December, after several battles, the Texas Army forced Cos to retreat from Texas.

On March 2, 1836, fifty-nine Texas leaders formally declared independence from Mexico. They wrote and adopted a constitution for their new Republic of Texas and created a temporary government. They elected David Burnet as president and placed Samuel Houston in charge of the army.

▼ Santa Anna freed the civilians—a few women, children, and slaves—before attacking the Alamo. Much of the information about the battle comes from these survivors.

The Alamo and Goliad

When Santa Anna heard of his son-in-law General Cos's defeat, he determined to avenge his family's honor and place Texas firmly under Mexican control. He arrived in Texas with a large army of about six thousand in January 1836. Some Tejanos—loyal to Mexico and not the new Anglo republic—joined Santa Anna's army, and it grew to about eight thousand.

Santa Anna wanted to control both roads into Texas from Mexico—one near San Antonio and one near Goliad. He sent some troops to

Battle for the Alamo

The battle for the Alamo is one of the most famous war stories of all time. The Texans bravely fought rather than surrender, and they managed to hold off an army of thousands with only about one hundred ninety men. The battle has come to represent courage and perseverance against great odds.

Some legendary Old West heroes died in the battle, including Davy Crockett, a Tennessee native known for his hunting, fighting, and storytelling skills. Jim Bowie—an adventurer known for his famous knife—also died defending the Alamo. The Spanish burned their bodies, and their burnt remains were later collected and buried with honor by Texans.

San Antonio Commandant Colonel Juan N. Seguín gave this speech to honor those killed in the Alamo: "Companions in Arms!! These remains which we have the honor of carrying on our shoulders are those of the valiant heroes who died in the Alamo. Yes, my friends, they preferred to die a thousand times rather than submit themselves to the tyrant's yoke. What a brilliant example! . . . I invite you to declare . . . 'Texas shall be free and independent or we shall perish in glorious combat.'"

Goliad under the command of General José de Urrea, and Santa Anna commanded the troops heading to San Antonio.

Mexico's first target was the Texas revolutionaries—including William Travis, Jim Bowie, and Davy Crockett—who were gathered at the San Antonio de Valero Mission, known today as the Alamo. For twelve days, from February 23 to March 6, Santa Anna's army surrounded the Alamo. Then, on unlucky day thirteen, he sent one thousand eight hundred troops to attack the crumbling fort walls. All one hundred ninety of the fighting men in the Alamo died defending it, and an estimated four hundred Mexican soldiers died capturing it.

In March, General Urrea captured Goliad for Mexico. Santa Anna had decreed that all foreigners who raised arms against Mexico were to be killed. On March 27, 1836, Santa Anna had Spanish firing squads massacre more than four hundred Texan soldiers.

News of the Alamo and Goliad defeats caused panic among Anglo Texans. Sam Houston retreated with his army and instructed settlers to follow. The settlers fled from their homes in what became known as the Runaway Scrape. Entire Anglo settlements were deserted and left unprotected from Mexican troops and Native American groups. Many settlers died of disease, cold, or hunger before reaching safety.

San Jacinto

▲ This 1890 painting by William Henry Huddle shows Santa Anna surrendering to Texas troops. One Texan who participated in the Battle of San Jacinto noted that the Texans had the Mexicans "running like turkeys" in only eighteen minutes.

Although many settlers fled, news of the fate of their comrades in arms at the Alamo and Goliad inspired the Texas Army to fight. "Remember the Alamo! Remember Goliad!" became Houston's cry to motivate the troops.

On April 21, 1836, in a surprise attack during siesta time, Houston led his Texas Army of about nine hundred against Santa Anna's army of about one thousand two hundred in the Battle of San Jacinto. Houston's troops killed, captured, or scattered the entire Mexican Army in about eighteen minutes. It was a great victory—only nine Texans died in the battle. The next day, Texas troops captured Santa Anna and forced him to withdraw his troops from Texas.

Santa Anna signed a public peace treaty that provided for prisoner exchange and property return and asserted the independence of Texas. A secret treaty promised the release of Santa Anna if he forced the Mexican government to honor the public treaty.

Texas Republic

The new Republic of Texas faced challenges to its survival. Even though Santa Anna signed treaties after the Battle of San Jacinto, other Mexican leaders still felt Texas was a part of Mexico and that Anglos had no right to declare independence. Mexico's congress voted to declare that Santa Anna's treaties were not valid and ordered the war to continue.

Government Structure

Anglo Texans quickly established a permanent government to deal with their country's problems. In addition to the threat of Mexican attack, Texas had few roads, poor communication between settlements, and no postal system. The government was already $1.25 million in debt from the war, and many people were poor. Settlers

◀ Sam Houston, first Texas president (1836–1838), had lived with the Cherokee and was adopted by a Cherokee Chief. He worked to secure treaties for Native Americans throughout his life.

◀ Much of the Texas frontier was dry, desertlike land, making farming and surviving difficult. The search for water was a constant problem. These men in Encinal, Texas, use mules and a barrel to transport water from the river toward home.

had returned home after the Runaway Scrape to find their livestock and possessions gone and their houses burned by the Mexican Army.

The temporary government held elections in September 1836. Texans elected two war heroes—Sam Houston and Mirabeau Lamar—as president and vice president for the first term (1836–1838). Voters also approved the pro-slavery constitution and were in favor of joining the United States.

The Texas government had three branches—an executive branch, consisting of a president and his advisors, a judicial branch headed by a supreme court, and a two-house legislature with representatives elected by Texans. The president served a three-year term and could not serve two consecutive terms.

Sam Houston's Native American Policy

Native Americans and settlers in Texas often came into conflict, as settlers took more and more land from American Indians. The Indians retaliated with raids on settlements and sometimes took

▲ The Texas Rangers were first formed in 1823 by Stephen Austin to protect his settlers from Indian raids. The rangers did their job, often in a fashion that brutalized Native people. Today, the rangers are a Texas state law enforcement agency. The rangers pictured here are patrolling the Texas-Mexico border in 1915.

prisoners. On May 19—less than one month after the battle of San Jacinto—Caddo and Comanche warriors attacked Fort Parker, taking two women and three children prisoner. The new Texas government felt it did not have enough resources to deal with the attack, but the Texas Army disagreed.

President Houston was in favor of forming treaties with Native Americans instead of fighting them. He believed "natural reason will teach them the utility [value] of our friendship."

Many soldiers, however, thought Houston's government was being too lenient. Colonel Rodgers, a military leader, urged his troops to march on the government, to "kick Congress out of doors, and give laws to Texas." President Houston had to disband the army to avoid military uprisings and civil war.

To achieve a safe frontier without the military, President Houston relied on a law enforcement group called the Texas Rangers. He also sent peaceful messages to the Native American groups living in Texas, including the Shawnee, Cherokee, and Comanche. He signed treaties granting land rights to Native Americans and built trading posts.

Mirabeau Lamar's Presidency

In 1838, Mirabeau Lamar was elected president and took office in 1839 (1839-1841). President Lamar was a poet, painter, and

Bleeding Under the Tomahawk

—President Lamar gave this speech in 1839 to ask for volunteers to fight Native American groups in the Texas frontier.

"Fellow Citizens, I am forced by the suffering conditions of our North Western frontier, to make an appeal to your valor and patriotism, which have never been appealed to in vain. The fierce and perfidious savages are waging upon our exposed and defenceless inhabitants, an unprovoked and cruel warfare, masacreing [sic] the women and children, and threatning [sic] the whole line of our unprotected borders with speedy desolation. All that a brave and energetic people could achieve for their own safety has been nobly done. They have met their enemies with unflinching hearts, and have borne their trials and reverses with a fortitude equaled only by their heroism. But their population, thinned by repeated and continued losses, are no longer able to sustain themselves against the overwhelming numbers by which they are surrounded; and if immediate relief be not intended, they will be compelled to break up their settlements, and seek security in our more populous counties. . . . Are you, citizen soldiers, willing to repose quietly at home while your countrymen and brethren are bleeding under the tomahawk, and their families are the unresisting victims of the scalping knife? Can you sleep upon your pillow, with the voice of lementation [sic] in your ears? Are you insensible to noble deeds—too timid for danger? No. Such is not the character of Texans."

visionary who was the first to set aside land for public schools. This earned him the nickname "Father of Texas Education."

One of President Lamar's goals was to have Mexico recognize Texas's independence. He asked the governments of the United States and Great Britain to help negotiate with Mexico. When negotiations failed, President Lamar decided to support the Yucatán, a Mexican frontier province, in its attempt to win independence from Mexico. He rented the ships of Texas's navy to the Yucatán to help with the war effort.

Another goal of President Lamar's was to eliminate Native Americans from Texas. He believed that "the proper policy to be pursued towards the barbarian race, is absolute expulsion from the country . . . the white man and the red man cannot dwell in harmony together. Nature forbids it." Lamar gained approval

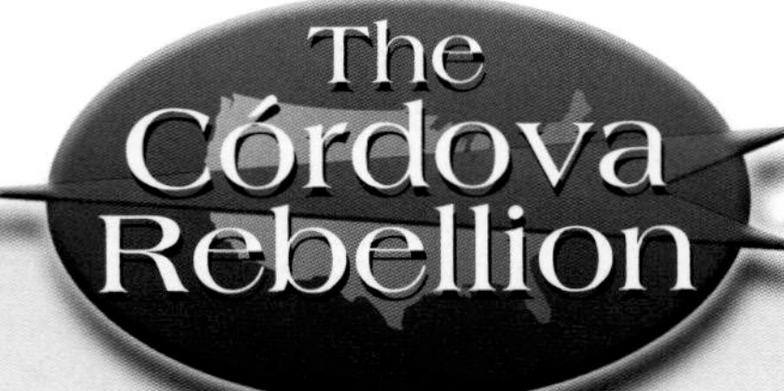

The Córdova Rebellion

Many people in the new Texas Republic were still loyal to Mexico. Vincente Córdova, an official in the former Mexican government of Nacogdoches, was one of them. Since 1835, he had worked for Mexico to "foster the favorable feelings which the faithful Mexicans here have always entertained."

In 1838, Córdova gained the support of the Cherokee for Mexico. The Cherokee had tried with no success to gain title to their lands—first from Mexico and then the Texas Republic. Córdova drafted a treaty that promised the Cherokee title to their hunting grounds and other privileges.

He gathered with the Cherokee and a large group of Mexican supporters near Nacogdoches in August 1838 and declared their support of Mexico. In response, Major General Thomas Rusk asked for local Texans to volunteer for a militia to fight Córdova's force. On September 16, Córdova led an attack on the volunteer militia, but he lost the battle, and the rebellion had ended by March 1839.

from the Texas congress to build military forts in the frontier and to form military units to engage American Indian forces.

In 1839, Texas forces killed Manuel Flores, a Mexican secret agent sent to recruit Native groups to align with Mexico against Texas. The Texas Rangers found papers that made Lamar fear the Indians would side with Mexico, and he ordered the rangers to force the Cherokee from Texas. The rangers also went on to cruelly remove the Shawnee, Alabama, and Coushatta from their hunting grounds and relocated them to eastern Texas. Then, in 1840, President Lamar launched a bloody war with the Comanche.

Santa Fe Expedition

President Lamar wanted to build Texas into a great empire that expanded to the Pacific Ocean. He did not want Texas to join the United States and even tried to claim more of Mexico's territory for Texas.

On December 1836, Texas's government had claimed land in New Mexico. Texas had hoped to tax merchandise caravans traveling along the popular Santa Fe Trail, thus bringing much-needed money into the republic's treasury.

▲ Texas president Mirabeau Lamar was born in Georgia and moved to Texas in 1835. He fought in the Texas Revolution and later for the United States in the Mexican-American War. In his later years, he lived on a plantation he bought in Richmond, Texas.

Houston had made no effort to enforce the Texas government's claim on Santa Fe, but Lamar did. Without the approval of the Texas congress, President Lamar wrote a letter to the people of Santa Fe on April 14, 1840, urging them to unite with the Texas Republic. He gave the letter to a commissioner from Santa Fe and organized a caravan of merchants and a military escort to accompany him. Twenty-one wagons carried supplies for the three hundred twenty-one members of the group and about $200,000 worth of goods to trade.

The expedition, unfortunately, lost its way, so the trip over steep mountains, arid plains, and raging rivers took much longer than expected. The group suffered from lack of water and food. When they finally reached New Mexico, Mexican troops were waiting to arrest them. They were marched hundreds of miles, from Santa Fe to a Mexico City jail. Any who fell behind had their ears cut off and were shot. Many Texans blamed President Lamar for the horrible failure of the expedition.

Texas Annexation to the United States

President Lamar's policies were expensive—the Comanche war alone cost about $2.5 million. During his term, Texas's national debt increased from about $3.25 million to $8 million. He issued paper money that quickly lost value.

In the 1841 election, Texans elected Houston to a second term as president (1841–1844). He promised to cut government costs and improve the Texas economy so that "Texas will again lift its head and stand among the nations. It ought to do so, for no country upon the globe can compare with it in natural advantages."

◀ Quanah Parker (pictured here sometime between 1909 and 1932) was the last Comanche chief to fight the Texans. Parker's band of Comanches held the plains of Texas uncontested for seven years in the 1800s.

▲ President Lamar issued paper currency in an attempt to help Texas's economy, but the money quickly lost value. At its lowest point, the Republic of Texas's currency was worth just 2 cents for every U.S. $1.00.

Instead of fighting them, President Houston made treaties with the Comanche and other American Indian groups. He cut spending by disbanding the military, bringing the navy's ships back from the Yucatán, and cutting government offices and salaries. He also renewed annexation talks with the United States.

U.S. Relations with Texas

Texas-U.S. relations began shortly after the Texas Revolution. Before officially recognizing Texas, U.S. president Andrew Jackson sent a State Department official to Texas to gather information. The official reported that it was doubtful if Texas could stay independent from Mexico because of its large debt and small population. At the time, about 30,000 Anglo Americans, 3,478 Tejanos, 14,200 Native Americans, and 5,000 slaves lived in Texas. Support of the American public, however, overrode the official's opinion, and Congress officially recognized Texas on March 3, 1837.

Texas had also proposed being annexed to the United States. The U.S. Congress, however—fearing war with Mexico, international disapproval, and internally divided about adding another slave state to the Union—fiercely debated about the

▲ Editorial cartoon illustrating annexation debate between 1844 U.S. presidential candidates. James Polk, who supported annexation, holds the hand of the lady, representing Texas. George Dallas, Polk's vice presidential choice, speaks in support of Texas. Henry Clay crosses his arms in symbolic rejection of annexation. Quaker represents abolitionists who did not want Texas to be a slave state.

issue. Texas withdrew its offer in 1838 because Congress kept postponing making a decision about annexation.

World Relations

Texas needed the income that trade with other countries would bring, so beginning in 1837, Texas leaders sent agents to France, Great Britain, Belgium, and the Netherlands.

Some world leaders were hesitant to loan money or sign treaties with Texas because they believed it would not stay independent. France, however, was at war with Mexico, so French officials eagerly signed a treaty recognizing the Texas Republic in 1839. The Netherlands signed a treaty on September 15, 1840.

In 1840, the United States and Great Britain were disputing the rights to the Oregon Territory, and it seemed as if the countries might go to war. If they did, Great Britain would no longer receive cotton imports from the United States and would need cotton from Texas. So, in November 1840, Great Britain recognized Texas independence and signed a trade treaty.

The Texas Rangers are one of the most famous law enforcement agencies of all time. The volunteer rangers first began work in the 1820s to protect Austin's settlers from Native American raids. In 1835, the Texas Rangers became an official agency, and rangers received a salary for their duties, which included policing the frontier against Native Americans and Mexican bandits.

After Texas became a state, the rangers became a volunteer group again. Several ranger units fought bravely during the Mexican-American War, helping to win major battles. This gave the group fame and recognition around the United States. Less publicized were the brutal raids and massacres that rangers conducted in Mexican towns and Native American settlements.

Despite its questionable past, the rangers were reorganized and made an official agency in 1874.

Mexican Invasion

In 1841, after Houston's election and after Santa Anna regained power in Mexico, Mexican leaders renewed their interest in reclaiming Texas. Santa Anna sent Mexican troops to Texas territory in January 1842. Texans and Mexican troops fought several battles, and on September 11, the Texans surrendered San Antonio. Fifty-two Texas prisoners were marched to jail in Mexico City.

Texans were furious and wanted revenge. At least seven hundred fifty men rushed to San Antonio and formed a volunteer army. General Alexander Somervell took command, and the army crossed the border and captured Laredo. Some Texas troops looted and destroyed the town. Other soldiers, upset with the looting, returned to Texas. The rest moved on

to fight and captured the Mexican town of Guerrero in December.

Somerville then ordered the troops home, but about three hundred refused and stayed in Mexico. Mexican forces captured them in Mier on December 26 and marched them to jail in Mexico City. Some escaped and were recaptured. Mexican officials ordered that a certain number be killed to teach them a lesson. Mexican troops forced the prisoners to pick beans from a bag. The seventeen Texans that drew black beans were shot and killed. The survivors were imprisoned, and many died in jail.

▲ Once Santa Anna regained power in Mexico, he decided to assert Mexico's rights over the Texas territory he had lost after the Battle of San Jacinto.

Annexation

In 1843, Santa Anna agreed to a proposal that Texas rejoin Mexico as an independent department, with the freedom to make its own laws and be represented in Mexico's congress. Santa Anna and President Houston then declared an armistice on June 15, 1843, to give Texas leaders time to evaluate the proposal.

Meanwhile, relations between Great Britain and Texas grew even friendlier. Great Britain began negotiating with Mexico to recognize Texas independence because it did not want Texas to join the United States. Great Britain believed the United States would be too powerful if it were allowed to gain more territory.

Officials in the United States disapproved of Great Britain's influence in Texas. They worried that Texas might become a satellite of Great Britain, putting the southern U.S. border in jeopardy. To avoid this, U.S. president John Tyler reopened annexation talks with President Houston. They drafted a treaty of annexation in June 1844, but the U.S. Congress did not approve it.

That same year, James Polk ran for U.S. president with an expansionist agenda. He won the election with his slogans the "Re-Annexation of Texas" and the "Re-Occupation of Oregon." Polk's victory convinced lame-duck president Tyler that the public supported the annexation of Texas, so before he officially left office, Tyler tried again.

Congress passed former President Tyler's annexation resolution on February 28, 1845. The terms were generous—Texas would immediately be a state, and slavery would be allowed. Texas could keep and dispose of its public land and had to pay the public debts of the Republic of Texas.

▲ John Tyler was President Harrison's vice president and assumed the role of president after Harrison died in office. He tried to annex Texas two times during his presidency and finally succeeded just before he left office.

Great Britain rushed to stop this annexation and quickly formed a deal with Mexico. Mexico agreed to recognize Texas's independence as long as Texas agreed not to annex itself to any other country.

Texans, however, believed being part of the United States would improve their economy and protect them against invasion by Mexico or other foreign forces. On June 16, 1845, Texas's congress voted to reject Mexico's peace plan and accept annexation to the United States. On July 4, a convention of Texas delegates passed an ordinance to approve annexation.

Texas State Government

Before Texas could become an official U.S. state, it had to draft a constitution and organize a state government for the U.S. Congress to approve. Texans completed these tasks at the Convention of 1845.

Convention of 1845

Texans elected fifty-seven delegates to attend the Convention of 1845. From July 4 to August 28, the delegates organized the Texas state government and wrote a constitution. Several items made the Texas constitution unique. All free Texas men were eligible to vote, unlike in many other states where only those men who owned property could vote. It was also the first state to protect the rights of women, married and single, to own property. Everyone was taxed equally, and state debt was limited to $100,000

◀ African American workers picking cotton in Texas around 1900. After slavery was outlawed, free African Americans had difficulty finding jobs. Many Texans took low-paying work doing what they had done as slaves—tending cotton.

except in special circumstances, such as invasion. The constitution set aside 10 percent of taxes to fund public schools.

A bill of rights guaranteed that Texas citizens would have freedom of press, religion, assembly, and the right to a trial by jury. Texas, however, allowed slavery to continue. African Americans and Native American rights were not recognized.

Government Structure

The state government remained divided into the same executive, legislative, and judicial branches as had existed in the Texas Republic's government. The head of the executive branch, however, was a governor rather than president. The governor had to be thirty years old and a resident of Texas for three years. Once elected, he served a two-year term.

The legislative branch consisted of a house of representatives with from nineteen to thirty-three members and a senate of

▼ There were few judges in the West, and lawlessness ran rampant. Still, Judge Roy Bean held court in this saloon on the Rio Grande and became known as the "Law West of Pecos." Bean once fined a dead man $40 for carrying a concealed weapon.

forty-five to ninety members. Senators served four-year terms, and representatives served two years. All members of Congress had to be at least thirty years old. None could be ministers or ever have participated in a duel.

The Supreme Court was the highest court in Texas followed by district courts. The governor appointed three judges to the Supreme Court for six-year terms.

▼ Anson Jones was the last president of the Republic of Texas. He was upset that he never regained a public office and killed himself in 1858.

Statehood

After Texas submitted its constitution to the U.S. Congress, Congress debated for weeks about adding Texas as another slave state. The desire for westward expansion, however, proved stronger than antislavery sentiments, and the Texas constitution was finally approved on December 29, 1845. Texas was an official state.

The Republic of Texas that had lasted for almost ten years ended on February 19, 1846, when newly elected Governor James Pinckney Henderson assumed control of the state government. The flag of the republic was lowered, and the U.S. flag was raised above it. As Texas president Anson Jones formally left office, he said, "The final act in this great drama is now performed; the Republic of Texas is no more."

Texas Public Lands

Texas was the only state allowed to keep its public land once it joined the Union. With millions of acres available, the sale of land was a main source of the state's income. The Constitution of 1845 kept in place many of the land principles that existed under the Republic of Texas. Texas soldiers were given land for service in the army, and land was given to companies as payment for completing improvement projects, such as building roads, railroads, or canals.

To attract settlers, the Republic of Texas had given away about 37 million acres (15,000,000 ha) in headright grants. These grants entitled all heads of households, except American Indians and African Americans, to receive land.

After the Mexican-American War ended in 1848, what is now New Mexico and Texas had a boundary disagreement. Texas insisted that the Rio Grande be its boundary and so claimed part of what is now eastern New Mexico to Santa Fe. New Mexicans, however, disagreed with Texas and refused to submit to the authority of its state government. The U.S. federal government wanted to solve the conflict, and Congress argued about the boundary issue for several years.

In 1850, Congress passed a compromise—the United States would buy the about 67 million acres (27 million ha) in question from Texas for $10 million, part of it in bonds. Texas used the money to pay its debts from its republic era. The land Texas sold eventually became parts of the states of New Mexico, Kansas, Wyoming, and Colorado.

The Republic also issued colonization contracts. One contract authorized six hundred French families to settle near the Medina and Frio Rivers. Another contract settled one thousand Dutch, German, Swiss, Danish, Swedish, and Norwegian families between the Llano and Colorado Rivers. Settlers from around the world made Texas a culturally diverse place. Each year the Republic of

More flags have flown in Texas than in any other state. The first flag was Spanish (1519–1685), and the second flag was French (1685–1690). Spain reclaimed the territory and flew its flag over Texas again (1690–1821). After winning independence, the Mexican flag (1821–1836) became the third to fly in Texas. The fourth flag was for the Republic of Texas (1836–1845). The Stars and Stripes of the United States was fifth, from 1845 to 1861. When Texas seceded from the Union and joined the Confederate States of America (1861), it flew the Confederate flag. After the Union defeated the Confederacy in 1865, Texas once again joined the United States and raised the Stars and Stripes.

Texas's state flag is the same design as the flag of its republic era. A blue vertical stripe covers one-third the width of the flag. A white, five-pointed star sits in the center of the blue stripe. The remaining two-thirds of the width consists of an upper white horizontal stripe and a lower red horizontal stripe.

Texas's population had increased by about seven thousand settlers. Even more emigrants swarmed into Texas once it became a state, and its population tripled by 1860.

State Capital

Texans had a difficult time agreeing on the location for their capital. The first elected government of the Republic of Texas met in Columbia for three months in 1836, then moved the capital to Houston in December of that year. Houston remained the capital until 1839.

In 1839, President Lamar proposed that Austin be made the new capital. This city was in the frontier, and its remote location fit well with Lamar's expansionist beliefs. He moved his administration and the government records to Austin in 1839.

Sam Houston was unhappy with the choice of Austin as the capital. He worried that, because it was on the frontier, Native Americans or Mexicans

▲ Construction of Texas's current state capitol (top left) in Austin began in 1882. It is the largest state capitol in the United States. Texas state senators meet in the Senate Chamber (middle right). Insets in the capitol floor (bottom right) honor Texas patriots who died at the Alamo and Goliad.

might attack and burn it. In his second term, in 1842, he ordered that the capital be moved back to Houston. He temporarily used Washington-on-the-Brazos as the government seat and ordered Texas Rangers to retrieve the archives from Austin.

Austin residents, however, wanted the capital to remain in their city, and they warned they would fight anyone coming for the archives. Houston did not want bloodshed. In a surprise move, the Texas Rangers quickly loaded the papers in wagons and left town. Austin was unprepared to resist, but its residents pursued the rangers and recaptured the archives. The struggle became known as the Archive War.

After Texas became a state, Texas residents voted on the site of their capital. Austin won by a large majority and is still the state capital today.

The Lone Star State

The United States assumed responsibility for the border dispute with Mexico after Texas became a state. In 1845, President James Polk sent John Slidell to Mexico to negotiate a formal border for Texas and to buy California and New Mexico. Mexican officials refused to talk to Slidell, and he left the country in August 1846, without accomplishing his mission.

Since Mexico refused to negotiate, President Polk sent American troops to the northern banks of the Rio Grande. Mexico interpreted the U.S. troop movements as an act of war. On April 24, 1846, about two thousand Mexican troops crossed the river and killed or wounded sixteen American scouts.

When President Polk received news of the Mexican attack, he asked that Congress declare war because "Mexico has passed the boundary of the United

◀ During the Mexican-American War, U.S. troops fought on foreign soil for the first time. This 1848 illustration recreates the entry of the U.S. Army into Mexico City.

States, has invaded our territory and shed American blood upon the American soil." The Mexican-American War (1846–1848) was the first U.S. war fought on foreign soil, and about seventy-five thousand men from around the United States volunteered to fight for their country, including five thousand Texans.

Mexican-American War

The first two battles of the war took place in Texas. Mexican troops crossed the Rio Grande and blocked a road at Palo Alto. General Taylor, commander of U.S. troops, needed to use the road to relieve a nearby fort. Both sides blasted each other's troops with artillery. The Mexican troops retreated to a more protected position, and the Americans claimed a victory.

The second battle took place the next day at Resaca de la Palma. Fighting was long and bloody, but American troops held their position, and the Mexican army retreated to Matamoros, Mexico. U.S. troops pursued and occupied Matamoros on May 18, 1846.

In the following months, U.S. forces captured more cities in Mexico, including Vera Cruz, Monterey, and Buena Vista. On September 16, 1847, the United States achieved its most

▼ An 1846 lithograph of the Battle of Palo Alto in Texas. In the battle at Resaca de la Palma, soldiers would fight from "resacas," dried up riverbeds that form trenches.

The U.S. Army & Native Americans in Texas

The U.S. government assumed a harsh policy toward Texas's Native Americans. In other areas of the United States, federal agents had signed peace treaties promising large reservations for Native Americans far from Anglo settlements. While this situation was far from ideal, at least the American Indians had somewhere to live. Federal authorities could not do this in Texas because the state government owned its public land, and Texas's congress only granted land for two small reservations on the Brazos River in 1854. The state government eventually forced even these Native Americans to relocate to Indian Territory, part of present-day Oklahoma.

In 1855, the U.S. Second Cavalry, created specifically to fight Native people in Texas, rode into the state. They conducted numerous scouting parties into Native territory and fought at least forty battles, killing hundreds of American Indians, mostly Comanches. By 1890, about 95 percent of the Native Americans in Texas had died from disease or war. Most of the survivors had been forced to relocate to reservations far from Texas.

important victory when it occupied Mexico City, the Mexican capital. After this defeat, Mexico decided to negotiate a peace settlement.

The war ended on February 2, 1848, when officials from both countries signed the Treaty of Guadalupe Hidalgo. In it, the United States agreed to give Mexico $15 million and to pay about $3.2 million worth of Mexico's debts. In return, Mexico agreed to recognize the Rio Grande border of Texas and to give nearly half its territory to the United States.

Native Americans and Forts

Throughout the recorded history of Texas, from its days under the Spanish, Mexican, Anglo Texan and U.S. governments, Native Americans had resented intrusions into their territory and fought to protect their land from foreign invaders. When it was a republic, Texas's congress had refused to formalize Indian treaties, so

▲ These Apache prisoners, including the famous warrior Geronimo (third from right in front row) and his son (second from left in front row), are resting near Nueces River, Texas, while being forcibly relocated to reservations by U.S. troops in 1886.

they never received legal title to their land. The Indians felt betrayed as increasing numbers of settlers took their land after Texas was annexed to the U.S.. To make matters worse, Anglo hunters began killing large numbers of buffalo, the animal Native Americans relied on for survival. Also, thousands of Natives died after being exposed to diseases carried by the settlers, such as cholera and smallpox. To retaliate for their loss of land and the deadly diseases, many Native groups raided settlements and took horses, livestock, and prisoners. Texas Rangers and U.S. troops then killed Native Americans and raided and burned their settlements for revenge.

To manage conflicts with the Native Americans, beginning in 1848 the U.S. Army built about forty-four new outposts and forts in Texas. About ninety soldiers lived in each fort. Soldiers at the forts tried to protect frontier settlers and the thousands of pioneers crossing Texas on their way to Santa Fe or California during the Gold Rush (1848–1850). Since the forts were far apart and understaffed, it was often difficult for soldiers to help those under attack.

The army spent money on forts, which helped nearby towns and the economy. Soldiers built roads and stagecoach lines from fort to fort. Merchants built general stores carrying supplies, and blacksmiths forged shoes for soldiers' horses. Local farmers sold crops to the soldiers. Hunters brought buffalo meat to towns, and ranchers raised cattle. One-room schoolhouses and churches served the growing population. By 1900, the forts had brought about $70 million of needed income to Texas.

Conclusion

The Aftermath of Manifest Destiny

Manifest Destiny was a romantic cause that inspired the developing United States. It created a feeling of nationalism as Americans rallied to spread democracy and conquer new territory. In the process, different regions of the country became interdependent on each other for goods. People began to think of themselves as Americans—working together to conquer a frontier.

One country's quest for progress, however, can often cause another's demise. Anglo settlers rejected and subjected other cultures because they felt the Anglo way of life was superior. The U.S. government broke treaties with Native Americans, killing them and stealing their land. Hundreds of soldiers died to advance U.S. boundaries and harshly imposed U.S. government on Native groups.

The annexation of Texas caused controversy. Some Americans felt that the Mexican-American War was an excuse to add pro-slavery territory to the United States. Other countries thought that the United States would be too powerful if it stretched from coast to coast.

Americans supporting Texas annexation reasoned that Mexico's claim to the territory was weak since only 1 percent of its population was Mexican. The ideal of Manifest Destiny convinced most Americans that they were saving Texans from the unstable Mexican government.

Texas did prove to be a valuable addition to the Union. One of Texas's main industries is ranching, and the hardy Texas longhorn became a staple food of households around the country during the cattle boom of the 1880s. Large supplies of minerals, such as oil, also enriched the state and supplied the country with valuable resources.

Today, Texas is proud of its unique and varied history. Texas's state flag is the same as the one flown while it was the Republic of Texas, and the single star on the flag gave the state its official nickname—"The Lone Star State."

1492: ▶ Columbus lands in the Americas and claims the land for Spain.
1682: ▶ The Spanish begin building missions in Texas.
1690: ▶ Ranching reaches the territory that would become Texas.
1803: ▶ The United States doubles its size with land bought in the Louisiana Purchase.
1810: ▶ Mexican Revolution begins.
1821: ▶ Mexico wins independence from Spain, and the Mexican Revolution ends.
1823: ▶ Empresario Stephen Austin forms the first large Anglo colony in Texas.
1824: ▶ Federalists take over Mexican government and write the Constitution of 1824.
1826: ▶ Fredonian Rebellion occurs when Haden Edwards separates from Mexico and forms the Republic of Fredonia after his empresario contract was canceled.
1830: ▶ Congress passes the Indian Removal Act, which legalized the removal and resettlement of Native American groups; Mexico passes the Law of 1830, which prohibits further Anglo settlement in Texas.
1832: ▶ Texans expel Mexican troops from several forts and write the Turtle Bayou Resolutions to explain their actions.
1834: ▶ Mexico passes a law ordering that missions be secularized.
1835: ▶ Texas Revolution begins with the Battle of Gonzales.
1836: ▶ Texans declare independence from Mexico; February 23-March 6-Santa Anna attacks the Alamo.
March 27—Mexican troops kill more than four hundred Texans in the Goliad Massacre.
April 21—Texans defeat Mexican Army at Battle of San Jacinto, thus ending the Texas Revolution.
September 5—Texans elect Sam Houston as first president of the Republic of Texas.
1837: ▶ The United States formally recognizes the Republic of Texas.
1839: ▶ Texans elect Mirabeau Lamar as Texas president.
1841: ▶ Texans elect Sam Houston to second term as president of the Republic of Texas.
1844: ▶ Texans elect Anson Jones as final president of the Republic of Texas.
1845: ▶ Texas becomes a state; John O'Sullivan first uses term Manifest Destiny.
1846: ▶ Mexican-American War begins.
1848: ▶ Mexican-American War ends when Treaty of Guadalupe Hidalgo is signed.
1850: ▶ California becomes a state.
1861: ▶ U.S. Civil War begins; Texas secedes from Union and joins Confederate States of America.
1865: ▶ U.S. Civil War ends.
1866: ▶ Texas rejoins the United States of America.

Anglo: person of non-Spanish, European descent

annexation: the adding of territory into an existing political unit, such as a nation, state, or county

armistice: a mutual agreement to temporarily end fighting

artillery: large-caliber weapons, such as cannons

ayuntamiento: an elected governing body who made laws and promoted local welfare, such as building roads

colony: area, settlement, or country owned or controlled by another nation

diverse: differing from one another; consisting of unlike characteristics, qualities, or elements

economy: system of producing and distributing goods and services

empire: political power that controls large territory, usually consisting of colonies or other nations

empresario: an immigration agent who has received a colonization contract from the Mexican government

frontier: edge of known or settled land

hacienda: a huge estate formed by a Spanish government land grant that is usually used for mining, ranching, or farming

manifest: obviously true and easily recognizable; the term Manifest Destiny meant that the "true and obvious" destiny of the United States was to expand its borders to the Pacific Ocean.

mestizo: person of Native American and Spanish descent

mission: center built to establish Spanish settlement, convert Native Americans to Catholicism, and exploit their slave labor

presidio: military fort built by the Spanish

province: district of a nation that usually has its own capital town and some form of local government, similar to states of the United States

rancho: Spanish word for ranch

republic: nation that has no sovereign or other unelected ruler but is led by a leader, or group of officials led by its citizens

secularize: make nonreligious

Tejano: a Texan of Mexican descent

trapper: hunter who uses traps to kill animals such as beavers or squirrels for their fur

treaty: agreement made between two or more people or groups of people after negotiation, usually at the end of a period of conflict

Books

Barenblat, Rachel. *Texas: The Lone Star State*. World Almanac Library of the States (series). Milwaukee: World Almanac Library, 2002.

Caravantes, Peggy. *An American in Texas: The Story of Sam Houston*. Notable Americans (series). Greensboro, NC: Morgan Reynolds Publishing, 2003.

Collier, Christopher, James Lincoln Collier. *Hispanic America, Texas and the Mexican War: 1835–1850.* Drama of American History (series). New York: Marshall Cavendish, 1998.

Egan, Tracie. *Francisca Alavez, the Angel of Goliad.* New York: Rosen Central Publishing, 2003.

Long, Cathryn J. *Westward Expansion.* History of the World (series). San Diego: Kidhaven Press, 2003.

Sipe, Antoinette Leonard. *The Alamo.* Philadelphia: Mason Crest Publishers, 2004.

Wade, Mary Dodson. *Texas History.* Chicago: Heinemann Library, 2003.

Web Sites

The Alamo
www.thealamo.org

The Handbook of Texas Online
www.tsha.utexas.edu/handbook/online/articles/view/HH/fho73.html

San Jacinto Museum of History
www.sanjacinto-museum.org

Texas Beyond History
www.texasbeyondhistory.net

Texas Online
www.state.tx.us

U.S.-Mexican War: An Online Resource
www.pbs.org/kera/usmexicanwar/

Index